MEDIEVAL HERALDRY

Text by
TERENCE WISE
Colour plates by
RICHARD HOOK
Line drawings by
WILLIAM WALKER

First published in Great Britain in 1980 by
Osprey Publishing, Elms Court, Chapel Way,
Botley, Oxford OX2 9LP,
United Kingdom.
Email: info@ospreypublishing.com

Also published as Men-at-Arms 99 *Medieval Heraldry*

ISBN 1 84176 106 0

Filmset in Great Britain
Printed in China through World Print Ltd.

FOR A CATALOGUE OF ALL BOOKS PUBLISHED BY OSPREY
MILITARY, AUTOMOTIVE AND AVIATION PLEASE WRITE TO:

The Marketing Manager, Osprey Direct USA,
PO Box 130, Sterling Heights, MI 48311-0130, USA.
Email: info@ospreydirectusa.com

The Marketing Manager, Osprey Direct UK,
PO Box 140, Wellingborough, Northants, NN8 4ZA,
United Kingdom.
Email: info@ospreydirect.co.uk

FRONT COVER: Rows of shields. (College of Arms, London, MS. Fenwick Roll)

BACK COVER: Arms of Edward IV. (College of Arms, London, MS. Vincent 152, p.53)

Visit Osprey at:
www.ospreypublishing.com

Introduction

It is not the aim of this book to describe in precise detail the rules of heraldry, but rather to introduce the reader to the rôle of heraldry and to provide examples of how it was used in the 14th and 15th centuries. Therefore, it is recommended that any reader lacking knowledge of the basics should have at hand an introductory book on the subject, such as the *Observer Book of Heraldry*, published by Warne.

It is anticipated that most readers of this book will be military enthusiasts, modellers and wargamers, and therefore I have concentrated on the purely military aspect of medieval heraldry. This is appropriate, as we are concerned here with a period of history during which heraldry retained one of its original functions—the identification of individuals and their followers on the field of battle. Matters such as mottoes, supporters, achievements, the arms of unmarried ladies, hatchments, and civil, ecclesiastical and corporate coats of arms have been omitted. Readers wishing to learn about these facets of the subject are referred to the Observer title, and to an interesting booklet entitled *Civic Heraldry*, published by Shire Publications. In place of these subjects readers will find more information on military matters, such as liveries, badges, crests, surcoats and horse trappers, than is normally found in books on heraldry.

Most books written by English authors almost totally ignore continental heraldry, and therefore an attempt has been made to include at least some European examples. However, almost inevitably the emphasis will be found to be on English heraldry, mainly because the various sources are more readily available to an English author, but also because drastic political changes in many European countries have caused the abolition of the Colleges of Heralds and the scattering or loss of their records. (The records of Polish medieval heraldry, for example, were destroyed during the Second World War.) It should also be remembered that most publications on European heraldry have not been translated into English, rendering much information inaccessible, for although many people can read French or German, and perhaps some Italian or Spanish, few can read Dutch, Polish, the Scandinavian languages, or medieval Latin.

English writers also usually overlook the fact that, once coats of arms had been adopted by the nobility, the lower orders in some European countries also began to assume coats of arms, and continued to do so until heraldry no longer had a

The effigy of John Eltham, Earl of Cornwall, in Westminster Abbey, *circa* 1334. He was the son of Edward II and bears the arms of England differenced by a bordure of fleurs-de-lys, his mother being Isabel of France. His shield is heater type.

Another form of shield which remained in continuous use throughout the medieval period was the pavise, which could be propped up to provide cover for an archer or crossbowman. It was normal to paint these shields, and this example bears the arms of the town of Zwickau: St George bearing a shield on which are painted three swans. It is dated *circa* 1480.

the nobility and *bourgeoisie* were not rigidly separated, but it should be remembered that the bearing of arms did not convert a *bourgeois* into a noble. Some 'nobles' were indeed *bourgeoisie*, but they had to be sure to state their origins. One definite form of distinction was that neither *bourgeoisie* nor peasantry were entitled to wear helmet crests.

Portugal and Germany were two other countries in which burghers and peasants were allowed to bear arms: in the latter even the Jews were permitted coats of arms, an unusually liberal practice in those days of rabid bigotry. Members of the lower classes in Portugal were forbidden the use of silver or gold in their arms, and in 1512 King Manuel I forbade the use of arms by all those not classed as nobles.

On Heraldry and Heralds

It is as well to begin by defining precisely what is meant by the word heraldry. Dictionaries usually refer to it as the art of the herald or, more helpfully, the art or science of armorial bearings, armoury being the medieval term for heraldry (Old French *armoirie*); but heraldry is perhaps best described as a system for identifying individuals by means of distinctive hereditary insignia, this system originating in western Europe during the Middle Ages. From archaeological sources we know that insignia have been used on the shields of warriors to identify individuals in battle since classical times—as early as *circa* 800 B.C. the Phrygians were using geometric and stylized floral designs on their shields—so what is it that makes medieval heraldry unique? The phrase 'distinctive *hereditary* insignia' contains the key, for all true heraldry is hereditary, that is the insignia are inherited without alteration by the heirs of the former bearers.

As far as can be ascertained, heraldry first appeared about the middle of the 12th century and flourished during the 13th and 14th centuries. The shapes of the shields used during these centuries made it necessary for the heralds and painters to adapt the natural forms used as insignia to fit irregular spaces, and the insignia therefore assumed a symbolic rather than natur-

purely military rôle. French sources quote many examples of *bourgeois* bearing arms in the 13th century, and by the end of that century this practice was widespread. From the *bourgeois* of the towns the bearing of arms spread to the peasants of the countryside, and the earliest known example of such arms in France occurs in 1369 (the arms of Jacquier le Brebiet—the shepherd: three sheep held by a girl).

Unlike the class system of England, in France

The effigy of a member of the Bowes family in the church of Dalton-le-Dale, Co. Durham, showing the tight-waisted jupon. The arms are another example of canting arms: Ermine, three bows bent and stringed, paleways in fess gules.

alistic appearance. Any study of heraldry soon reveals a considerable difference between the simple forms used in the early days and the more perfect and intricate forms of the later days. The almost ascetic style of the early years identifies the true medieval heraldry.

As more and more knights, and their sons, were granted the right to bear arms, so the insignia became by necessity more complex. However, by *circa* 1500 the original purposes for which heraldry had been introduced (on shields, surcoats, horse trappers and banners, to distinguish combatants in war and in tournaments, and on seals as marks of identity instead of signatures) were becoming obsolete. After the turn of the century the insignia began to be more and more complex, assuming naturalistic forms rather than the traditional symbolic ones. When this occurred, by about 1550, the era of true heraldry had ended and thereafter the science declined: seals were no longer so important because of the spread of literacy, and identification was now achieved on the battlefield by the use of flags, and in the tournament by the use of crests.

★　　★　　★

Coats of arms were at first used only by kings and princes, then by their great nobles. By the mid-13th century arms were being used extensively by the lesser nobility, knights and those who later came to be styled gentlemen, and, as mentioned above, in some countries the use of arms spread to merchants and townspeople, and even to the peasantry. Anyone who wished to have a coat of arms just invented one, though often it would be based on the arms of his overlord.

All these arms were assumptive arms, i.e. assumed without reference to any higher authority by the bearer in order to distinguish his person and property. This practice inevitably led to a certain amount of duplication of armorial bearings, and as more and more men assumed arms so matters became more confused.

Heralds had existed since possibly as early as 1132, but their duties in the beginning had consisted only of extolling the deeds of knights at tournaments. They were soon responsible for

5

proclaiming and organizing these tournaments, so popular in the 12th century, and consequently became heraldry experts whose job it was to identify the contestants by the insignia painted on their shields and banners. These heralds were more akin to minstrels at this date, wandering from country to country in pursuit of the tournaments, and so getting to know everyone of importance throughout Europe. From this familiarity with the great men of their time sprang their usefulness to military commanders, and medieval manuscripts mention heralds being present at the battles of Drincourt (1173) and Las Navas de Tolosa (1212), though there is no mention of heralds in royal service until the end of the 13th century.

The military value of men who could identify the contingents of an opposing army by the shields and banners of their lords speaks for itself, and almost every knight was soon employing a herald, no matter how small the force he commanded. The duty of these heralds was to be near their lord constantly (on campaign they lodged in their lord's tent) so as to be on hand to answer at once any query on the identity of a knight, and by the beginning of the 14th century this had caused their elevation from wandering minstrels to appointed officials and confidants of the nobles' households; by the middle of the century heralds in France and England had acquired a settled status. However, in Germany heralds were slow to acquire any official recognition and as late as at least 1338 no clear division existed between minstrels and heralds; a wardrobe account of that year records payments to the King of Heralds of Germany and ten *other* minstrels of Germany for making minstrelsy before the king at Christmas.

By the mid-14th century heralds were being continuously employed by the kings and princes of Europe, both in peacetime and in time of war. In fact their dual rôle as herald and envoy with diplomatic immunity was to become incompatible by the end of the century. A letter written *circa* 1400 by the Anjou King of Arms highlights the problem, for it deplores the way in which pursuivants (literally the rank below herald) abused their immunity to spy out the military plans of their master's enemies.

To mark their office heralds wore on their livery

An inn sign (the Tabard Inn in Gloucester) illustrating the form and decoration of the tabard of an English herald. Such examples of heraldry may be found all around us even today.

the arms of the lord they served. Later they were also to become responsible for organizing the marriages and funerals of the nobility, as well as other ceremonies and pageants. Nevertheless, despite their status and undoubted importance in all matters related to heraldry, until the late 14th century the English heralds at least had no control over the design of arms or who bore them, being responsible only for recording and identifyings the various coats of arms.

By the first quarter of the 14th century two trains of thought appear to have emerged concerning the use of armorial bearings: firstly, that such arms might be assumed by any man; and secondly, that the bearing of such arms must be the exclusive right of the nobility if heraldry was to function. The first known reference to a challenge over the right to bear particular arms occurs in a German document of 1286. In England the first such dispute was in 1348, before a Court of Law. This dispute was between Nicholas, Lord Burnell, and Robert, Lord Morley, and was tried by the Lord High Constable and Earl Marshal of England during the siege of Calais.

A more famous and prolonged case occurred between the years 1385 and 1390 when the Grosvenor, Scrope and Carminow families all claimed the ancient right to bear Azure, a bend or. No mention is made of heralds being involved in the allocation of these arms, or being involved in the dispute over them; the case was tried by the Court of Chivalry, a pre-heraldic court presided over by the Constable and Marshal, whose original rôles had been to deal with military matters and disputes affecting dignity and honour. Grosvenor won and Carminow conceded defeat, but Scrope appealed to the sovereign, Richard II.

Although heralds were not involved in this case, we know that from at least the 14th century the English Kings of Heralds (later called Kings of Arms) and their heralds were making surveys or collections of the existing arms within their provinces, and the case of Scrope v. Grosvenor may well have arisen from such a survey, which would have revealed the duplication of arms and called for a settlement. The English Kings of Arms at this time were Clarenceux, responsible for all England south of the Trent, and Norrey, responsible for all England north of the Trent. The anonymous Rolls of Arms which have been handed down to us were probably compiled by the early heralds and Kings of Arms when they were attempting to regularize English heraldry.

By the 15th century the Kings of Arms were required to take an oath on assuming office to the effect that they would do their utmost 'to have knowledge of all the noble gentlemen within their marches and them with their issue truly register such arms as they bear'.

The disputes mentioned above, and no doubt many others of shorter duration, made it necessary that some authority should be set up which could relieve the sovereign of the task of regulating the bearing of arms, assigning arms when applications were considered worthy, and preventing the unlawful assumption of those arms by others.

In France a College of Heralds was created in Paris by Charles VI in 1407, the head of this organization being known as Montjoie, King of

A pavise of *circa* 1490 bearing the arms of Ravensburg in Württemberg: Argent, a castle sable.

The Tudor badges of rose, portcullis, pomegranate and fleur-de-lys on the Houses of Parliament.

7

The rising sun badge of Edward III, still in use today as an inn sign.

King of Arms of Englishmen, whose province was the whole of England and Wales and who was responsible for issuing Patents of Arms for peers.

Shortly after these steps, Thomas, Duke of Clarence and brother to Henry V, appears to have issued ordinances which granted to the Kings of Arms the right to assign arms to persons within their provinces. The oldest known Patent issued by a King of Arms is dated 10 March 1439, and was issued by Sir William Bruges, first Garter King of Arms, to the Drapers' Company of London.

In 1484 Richard III by Royal Charter incorporated the College of Arms, or Heralds' College, which controls the use of armorial bearings in England (and Wales officially) to this day. The College of Arms is presided over by the Earl Marshal and apart from the three Kings of Arms it has six heralds—Somerset, Chester, Windsor, Richmond, Lancaster and York; and four pursuivants—Rouge Croix, Rouge Dragon, Portcullis and Bluemantle. The Court of Lord Lyon (King of Arms) in Scotland is in fact pre-heraldic. It has three heralds—Albany, Marchmont and Rothesay; and three pursuivants—Carrick, Unicorn and Kintyre. The office of Ulster King of Arms was instituted in 1553 and existed until 1940, when it was amalgamated with Norrey King of Arms. The office of Ireland King of Arms existed for a short period only prior to 1553.

In Portugal heralds were introduced during the reign of James I (1385–1433). A complete record of the arms of the nobility was drawn up in 1509 by the King of Arms, and Portuguese heraldry continued to be regulated by the heralds until 1910, when the monarchy was replaced by a republic.

German heralds were active and effective in the medieval period but had become extinct by the 1700s. It is significant that there was no word in the German language for herald until the Renaissance, the term *Knappen von der Wappen* (esquires of arms) being used instead. The German '*Knappen*' only broke from their wandering life by taking employment with the Tourney Societies, and in many German states the heralds never attained a position at court, the regulation of heraldry being handled by clerks under the court chancellor.

Arms, with ten heralds and pursuivants under him. We know Jacques de Heilly held the post of Montjoie at Agincourt nine years later, and wore the arms of France on his herald's coat. A *Maréchal d'Armes des Français* was appointed by Charles VIII in 1489. However, the French heralds were always strictly controlled by the king, who was the only person allowed to grant a coat of arms, while Parliament decided cases of heraldic disputes, thus relegating the heralds to the rôle of technical advisers. By the beginning of the 17th century the College had become totally ineffective and was abolished in 1792 owing to the Revolution, as was the science of heraldry itself. This has led to the anomaly of France, whose language is the language of heraldry, having no regulated system of heraldry today.

In 1417 Henry V of England sent Letters Patent to sheriffs of three counties declaring that 'whereas in recent expeditions abroad many persons had taken to themselves Arms and tunics of Arms called "Cotearmures" which neither they nor their ancestors had used in time past, no man of whatever rank should henceforth take arms unless he possessed them by ancestral right or by the grant of some person having authority sufficient thereunto'. That same year Henry created a new heraldic officer, Garter Principal

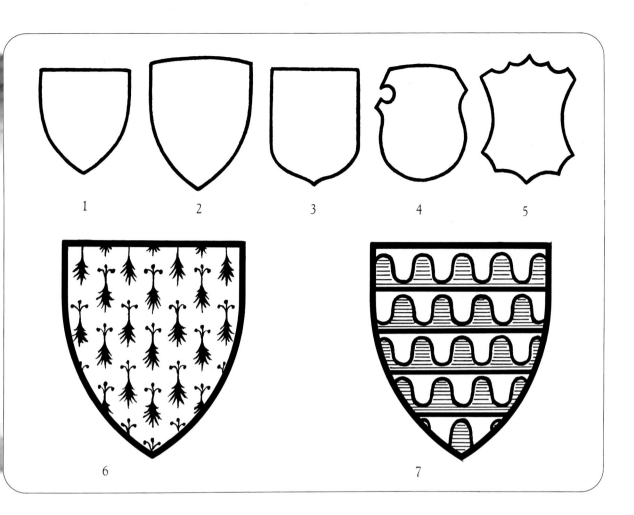

1   2   3   4   5

6   7

The Spanish heralds, like the French, seem to have been relegated to a secondary rôle by the kings of the various kingdoms, arms being granted by the kings and cases of duplication of arms being settled by the kings, the heralds playing only a consultant rôle. This was also the case in Denmark, where there was no official body of heralds, and arms were assumed or granted by the king by Letters of Patent.

The Shield

Because the shape and construction of the shield so clearly played an important part in the development of heraldic designs, it is necessary to take a brief look at the types of shields used in Europe during the period 1150–1550. The kite-shaped shield always associated with the Normans remained in use throughout the 12th century, when heraldry was evolving, but soon after the middle of the century the curved top was replaced by a straight one. Infantry continued to use this type of shield in Italy until as late as the 15th century. The kite shield was not flat, as it appears in books on heraldry, but semi-cylindrical, 'so as to embrace the person of the wearer'. This meant that not much more than half the shield could be seen from any one angle, and this greatly influenced the way in which insignia were placed upon the shield, since a man might need to be identified in battle or at the tourney by only half of his coat of arms.

At the beginning of the 13th century the kite shield was shortened to form what is now called the heater shield, so named in the 19th century because it resembled the base of the flat iron or heater then in general use. This shield, *Fig 1*, 13th century, and *Fig 2*, 14th century, also curved round the body for greater effectiveness. The heater was the commonest type of shield in most

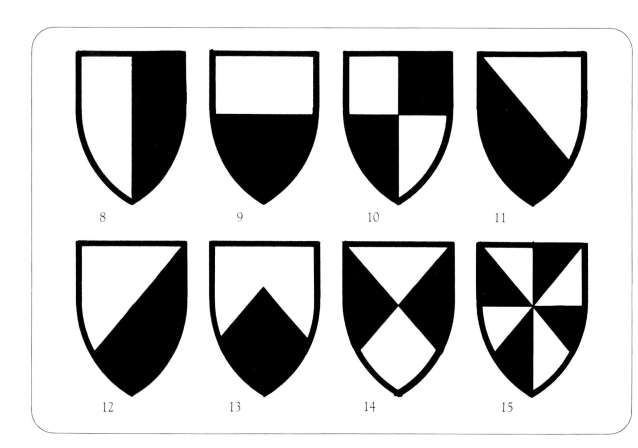

parts of Europe during the 13th and 14th centuries, but was unknown in Spain and Portugal. In these two countries shields were more rectangular, with a curved base, *Fig 3*, and this so influenced the number and placing of insignia in medieval times that the arms used in these countries often had their charges arranged in a completely different manner to other parts of Europe.

Shields had begun to diminish in size in the 13th century, as plate armour was introduced to protect arms and legs, and in the following century they were employed less frequently by mounted men as the use of plate armour increased. Thus the all-enveloping plate armour of the 15th century made shields obsolete for knights at least, and in the 1360–1400 period the shield gradually went out of use by knights in battle. By the 15th century knights rarely used the shield except for display purposes in parades and at tournaments. As a consequence the shields of the 15th century had more fanciful shapes, as shown by *Figs 4* and *5*. *Fig 4* shows a typical 15th-century tournament shield, called *à bouche*, the notch on the right side

being for the lance. *Fig 5* shows a purely decorative shield of the same century. Late 15th- and early 16th-century shields were of a similar design but often had a central ridge or a number of flutings at top and bottom. These more decorative shields became popular for ornamental purposes, particularly in architecture; but the simple lines of the 13th- and 14th-century shields remained popular for the display of heraldic art, and are still used in heraldry to this day.

In heraldry the face of the shield, on which the arms are painted, is known as the field or ground. In order to determine exactly whereabouts on the field the various colours and devices should be placed, and to be able to blazon a coat of arms correctly (that is to describe it verbally) the field is divided into a number of points. It is necessary here to know only that the top part of the field is called the chief, the central area the fesse, and the bottom the base. Because the shield is always viewed as seen from the position of the bearer, the dexter (right) side of the shield is that which coincides with the right side of the bearer, and the sinister (left) side is that which coincides with the

10

left side of the bearer.

Although I have already stated that it is not the intention of this book to describe the rules of heraldry, it is important that the reader be able to distinguish between those rules and practices which were particularly applicable in medieval times, and those which were not in use at this early stage. The next headings therefore provide brief summaries of the basics of heraldry as used in the 14th and 15th centuries.

Tinctures

The field of the shield and all devices painted upon it are coloured, and the different colours employed in heraldry are referred to as tinctures. In the medieval period the designs on shields were simple and the colours employed were bold, the aim being to create arms which were clearly visible and identifiable at a distance. The principal tinctures used are divided into metals (silver and gold), colours (red, blue and black), and furs, ermine *(Fig 6)* and vair *(Fig 7)*. Both the furs were based on furs in use at the time, ermine being the white winter coat of the stoat, with the black tips of the tails sewn on, and vair (from the Latin *varus*, various or varied) being the name given to squirrels' fur, much used for the lining of cloaks, which was bluish-grey on the back and white on the belly. As the coats of western European stoats do not normally turn white in winter, these skins had to be imported from as far away as Muscovy, at great expense, and were consequently used only by the great nobles, such as the Dukes of Brittany, whose coat was ermine.

The following table shows the colours, their heraldic name, and the abbreviation normally found on drawings of arms:

Tincture	Heraldic name	Abbreviation
Gold or yellow	or	O
Silver or white	argent	Arg or Ar*
Blue	azure	Az
Red	gules	Gu or G*
Black	sable	Sa or S*
Green†	vert	Vt or V*
Purple†	purpure	Purp or P*

*These contractions are normally used for tricking: see under Blazon.

†There was an antipathy towards green until well into the 15th century and although it occurs in arms as early as the 13th century, it was not in common use until the late 15th century. So far as purple is concerned, there was no distinction made between it and red in early medieval times and therefore we are not really concerned with it here.

As heraldry became established, more coats of arms were recorded and it became necessary to increase the tinctures in order to avoid duplication of arms. Thus by the 15th century tenné (orange) and murrey (a mulberry or reddish-purple colour) had been added to the colours. These new colours were mainly confined to continental heraldry, though they do occasionally appear on English flags or liveries; for example the livery colours of the House of York were murrey and azure, while the pages of the Earl of Nottingham wore tenné edged with sable during the reign of James I. The colour russet is also found on rare occasions in continental heraldry from the 15th century on, and appears in English heraldry on the flags and livery of the great Percy family.

The number of furs was also increased in the 15th and 16th centuries by depicting ermine and vair in different colours: ermines, white tails on black; erminois, black tails on gold; pean, gold tails on black. Vair was termed vairié if colours other than argent and azure were used: for example, vairié of or and gules.

Divisions of the Shield

In addition to the tinctures there are also several

Another example of ancient heraldry still being used—the white hart badge of Richard II as an inn sign.

methods of dividing the field by a single line in order to increase the number of coats of arms possible without duplication. A field thus divided is described as 'parted' or 'party', although the word party is often omitted in blazon. There are eight main divisions of this nature: per pale, fess, bend (dexter and sinister), chevron, saltire, quarterly, and gyronny. These divisions have been illustrated for clarity and appear in the order listed: *Figs 8–15*. In the early days of heraldry 'party' meant simply the division of the field per pale, and other division lines had to be named in full.

Continental, and particularly German heraldry contains many other field divisions unknown in England. One of the divisions most commonly used, especially in Italy and Germany, is a tripartite division of the field by two lines running horizontally, vertically, diagonally from top left, or diagonally from top right, across the shield. These are referred to as tierced in fess, pale, bend and bend sinister respectively. *Fig 16* illustrates tierced in fess, the arms of the Venetian family of Franchi; and *Fig 17*, tierced in bend, the arms of the Amici family, also Italian. Another variant of this style is tierced in pairle, best described by the illustration of the arms of the Saxon family of von Briesen, *Fig 18*. Another curious partition, unique to Germany, is that of tierced in gyron gyronnant, known in German heraldry as *Schneckenweise*. This is illustrated by the arms of the von Megenzer family, *Fig 19*.

The divisions known in English heraldry are also occasionally employed in a different form on the Continent. Quarterly, for example, sometimes appears as a most curious arrangement, best described by *Figs 20* and *21*, the arms of the Brunswick family of von Tule and the Löwenstein family respectively. Party per fess in German heraldry sometimes has a left or right 'step', known as *mit linker stufe*. This is illustrated by the arms of the Aurberg family of Bavaria, *Fig 22*. Other continental partition lines are difficult to blazon in English, nor can they really be categorized. Examples of these unusual divisions are shown in *Figs 23–27*, the arms of Lang von Langenau, Stauffeneck, Marshalck von Stuntsberg, Kirmreitter, and Altorf.

Varied fields are made by further divisions

which always consist of an even number of pieces, for example, barry, bendy, paly, per pale and barry, paly wavy, chequey, lozengy, and fusily, illustrated in that order by *Figs 28–35*.

Partition Lines

So far it has been assumed that all the lines dividing the field are straight, but in fact irregular partition lines were soon introduced to provide scope for more coats of arms. In the very earliest Rolls of Arms only three such variations are listed: Engrailed, Indented or Dancetty, and Undy or Wavy, and of these Engrailed was by far the most common. *Fig 36* illustrates the use of an engrailed line: Or, a cross engrailed sable, the arms of John de Bohun, temp. Edward I. *Fig 37* is Or, a chief indented azure, the arms of John Butler, Earl of Ormond, killed at Tewkesbury in 1471. Nebuly and Embattled (or Crenelle) were added later, within the period which concerns us here: *Fig 38*, Barry nebuly of 8, or and sable, the arms of Sir Humphrey Blount, 1422–77; and *Fig 39*, per fess embattled or and azure, the Barons von Preysing.

Charges

Charges are the devices used upon shields. In the 14th century by far the commonest types of charges were those listed in all books on heraldry as Ordinaries and Subordinaries. The Ordinaries are known as the Chief, Fess, Pale, Chevron, Bend, Saltire, Cross, Pile, and Quarter or Canton. The Chief is rare in Spanish and Portuguese arms. Each of these Ordinaries is illustrated here by a coat of arms: *Fig 40* (Chief) the arms borne by William de Fortz of Vivonne in France. *Fig 41* (Fess) the arms of Walter de Colville. *Fig 42* (Pale) the arms of Hugh de Grentmesnil, Lord of Hinckley, High Steward of England in the time of Henry I. *Fig 43* (Chevron) the arms of the French family of Gorrevod, Ducs de Pont de Vaux and

(16) **Franchi: chief vert, fess argent, base gules.** (17) **Amici: sinister chief or, bend gules, dexter base azure.** (18) **Von Briesen: dexter or, sinister gules.** (19) **Von Megenzer: the upper part of the shield is gules, the lower is or.** (20) **Von Tule: upper dexter and lower sinister divisions are gules.** (21) **Löwenstein: sable and or.** (22) **Aurberg: argent and sable.** (23) **Lang von Langenau: a 'chief' or, lozengy argent and gules.** (24) **Strauffeneck: a 'chief' argent, barry argent and gules.** (25) **Marshalck von Stuntsburg: gules, a 'chevron' argent.** (26) **Kirmreitter: sable and or.** (27) **Altorf: sable and argent.**

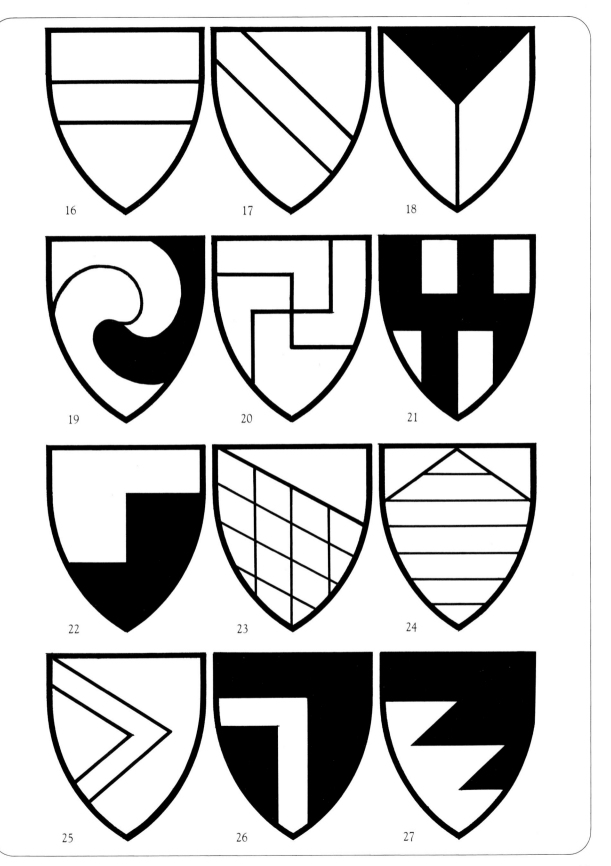

16

17

18

19

20

21

22

23

24

25

26

27

princes of the Holy Roman Empire. *Fig 44* (Bend) the arms borne by the French knight Guillaume de Trie. *Fig 45* (Saltire) the arms of the great house of Neville. *Fig 46* (Cross) the arms of the Portuguese family of Teixeira, also the Spanish family of Oluja. *Fig 47* (Pile) the arms of Sir John Chandos, Knight of the Garter, died 1370. *Fig 48* (Canton) the arms of Bertram de Crioll. Of these Ordinaries the most popular in the early period was the Fess and its diminutives, namely the Bar, Closet and Barrulet, which were almost always used in series; i.e. *Fig 49* Barry of 6, argent and azure, the arms of Henry de Grey of Codnor, who fought at Falkirk (1298) and at the siege of Caerlaverock in 1300. A Seigneur de Grey also bore these arms at the siege of Rouen in 1418.

In modern heraldry the Chief, Fess, Pile, Chevron, Bend and Pile all occupy one-third of the area of the field, but during the period with which we are dealing they were somewhat smaller, unless they bore a charge, and the Fess of ancient heraldry would now probably be termed a Bar. The Canton occupies a third of the Chief, always on the dexter side, except in Spanish heraldry, where it appears on either the dexter or sinister side.

The Subordinaries include the bordure, in-escutcheon, orle, tressure, flanches, gyron, lozenge, fusil, mascle, rustre, fret, billet, annulet and roundels: these may be found illustrated in any book on heraldry.

Next in popularity after the Ordinaries and Subordinaries came what are known as the animate charges, the various animals, with the lion rampant well ahead of all others, followed at a considerable distance by the lion passant. Less popular still in our period was the eagle, which was the most common charge in the bird category, and was followed by a relatively few examples of martlets, popinjays, crows, swans and herons.

The inanimate charges were mostly everyday objects from medieval life in Europe, such as staves, water buckets, arrows, axes, horseshoes, spurs, hammers, various flowers, stars and crescents, etc. It was not until around 1500 that the human body, monsters and fabulous beasts, birds and reptiles became common in heraldry, and by then the science had already begun its decline into ostentatious ornamentation.

Blazon

When a knight entered the lists at a tournament, he was announced by the sounding of a trumpet and the calling out of his coat of arms. This was known as blazoning. Thus the principal terms and order of description employed in blazon have been in existence since the early 13th century, by which date heralds were finding it necessary to describe a coat of arms in such a way that there could be no shadow of doubt as to what and whose it was, and they are readily understood throughout western Europe. The language of the early blazons was French or Latin, but this was later replaced by the language of each nation, and in English heraldry the language of blazon has become anglicized except for a few technical terms.

Some attention to fine detail has been applied in the following description of blazon, as it is essential that the reader be able to interpret blazon if he is to be able to study more complex books on heraldry, where the arms are frequently described in this manner. However, it should be remembered that blazon was invented in order

The reverse of the sixth Great Seal of Edward III, used between 1340 and 1372, showing shield, surcoat and trapper bearing the quartered arms of England and France, and the lion crest of the kings of England.

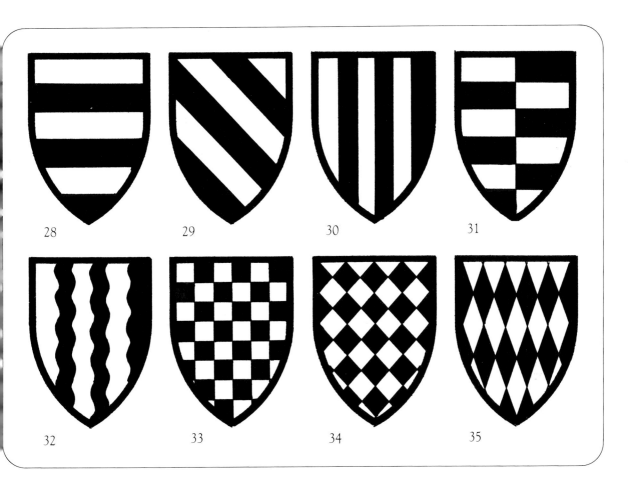

28   29   30   31

32   33   34   35

to describe arms precisely, clearly and briefly, and is therefore reasonably easy to understand.

To write or read a blazon it is necessary to know the order in which the description is set out. This order is therefore listed fully here.

The Field

(1) Describe the tincture of the field.

(2) If the field is divided into two or more tinctures, describe the line or lines which divide it, followed by the tinctures: Quarterly, or and gules, the arms of Sir Geoffrey de Say (baron 1313) and his son Geoffrey at the siege of Calais in 1348.

(3) If the partition lines are not straight, describe them: Per pale indented, argent and gules, the banner of Simon de Montfort.

(4) If the field is semé with small charges this must also be mentioned: Azure billety, a fess dancetty or, the arms of Sir John D'Eyncourt.

The Principal Charge

(1) Describe the principal charge on the field and its tincture.

(2) If the charge is an Ordinary and it has irregular lines, describe the lines—engrailed, nebuly, etc.

(3) If the charge is placed in the centre of the field and faces the dexter, no further description is necessary, otherwise the position (in chief, in fess, in base) and whether affronté (showing full face) or contourné (facing sinister) must be stated.

Other Charges

If there are any secondary charges these must be mentioned in order of importance, stating position on the shield and the tinctures used: Or, a cross gules between sixteen eaglets azure, the arms of the lords of Montmorency.

Charges upon Charges

Describe any charges placed upon an Ordinary, upon a principal charge, or upon a secondary charge.

Differences

Describe any charges used for differencing or cadency, such as the bordure, label, canton, crescent, mullet, etc.

Overall Charges

When an Ordinary is placed across a coat of arms

15

it is preceded by the word *surtout* or overall, i.e. overall a bend azure.

Quartering

If a shield is quartered this fact is stated before all the above categories, and mention is made at the end of this list only because quartering, except for royal alliances, was comparatively rare in the period with which we are concerned. Quarters are numbered 1 to 4 thus: top left, top right, bottom left, bottom right, as viewed. If the 4th quarter is a repeat of the 1st, and the 3rd a repeat of the 2nd, as in the arms of England *circa* 1400–1603, this is blazoned as Quarterly 1st and 4th France modern; 2nd and 3rd England.

The normal reading and writing rules of working from left to right and top to bottom apply in heraldry, so that per pale gules and or means the left side is red, and per fess argent and azure means the top half is argent. Gyronny commences with the top left-hand segment and the number of gyrons is stated: Gyronny of 8, or and sable, the arms of the Campbell family.

If a tincture is used more than once in a coat it is usual not to repeat its name but refer to it as 'of the first' or 'of the second', depending when it first occurred in the blazon. For example, in the Luterell arms the colour of martlets and bend is only mentioned once: Azure, a bend between 6 martlets or. This could equally be blazoned Azure, a bend or between 6 martlets of the second.

When a charge is repeated the number of such charges must be stated and their arrangement on the shield described. Thus nine roundels, 3, 3, 3. It is not necessary to blazon six roundels 3, 2, 1, as this is the standard arrangement for such a number of charges.

Correct punctuation is not vital and many authorities disagree over the way blazon should be punctuated, but it helps to remember that there should always be a comma after each tincture except where alternate colours are used, as in Barry of 6, argent and azure (de Grey).

The natural colouring of animals, birds, plants, etc., is always referred to as 'proper', but if they vary from their natural colours then the tinctures must be named. Birds and beasts having claws, beaks and teeth in a different tincture to that of their bodies are blazoned Armed. If their tongues protrude they are Langued. Animals such as the bull and unicorn, which also have horns and hooves, are blazoned Armed and Hoofed, but stags and deer are Attired, not Armed. Birds without claws are blazoned Beaked and membered. There are many more such complications, but the majority arose after the period with which we are dealing, when arms had become complex and heraldry was mainly decorative.

Tricking

There is another method of describing a coat of arms, found in Rolls of Arms dating back as far as the mid-13th century. In this method the coat is drawn in outline in ink and the various tinctures indicated by words or abbreviations of those words. Such a coat, known as tricked, is illustrated to indicate the simplicity of this method: *Fig 50*, the arms of Sir John Fortescue, *circa* 1394–1476. Neatness and accuracy are, of course, vital with this method to prevent confusion.

Surcoats

At the beginning of the 14th century it was common practice for knights to wear a surcoat over their armour. On the front and back of this coat would often be displayed their arms, though other heraldic devices might also be used: for example, Edward II of England (1307–27) wore four lions on his surcoat, while at Poitiers Sir John Chandos had the figure of Our Lady, dressed in blue, within a golden mandorla, embroidered on his surcoat. Lord Jean de Clermont, one of the French marshals at the battle, bore the same device on his surcoat.

At this date the surcoat was full length, reaching almost to the ankles, but sleeveless, and was split at front and back almost to the waist to allow the material to hang freely when the wearer was in the saddle. These gowns, typical examples of which are illustrated by *Figs 51* and *52*, were gathered at the waist by a belt or cord.

This full-length surcoat remained popular until about 1320–30, when the front skirts were cut off at mid-thigh level, as in *Fig 53*. This edge was sometimes straight, sometimes scalloped or embattled. Prior to this change, introduced for practical reasons, the ends of the front skirts had frequently been tucked through the belt to loop them up and so allow greater freedom of move-

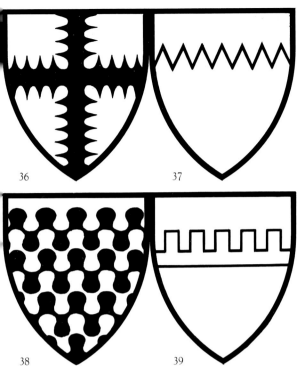

36

37

38

39

ment when on foot. Some examples of surcoats at about this date appear to have had the skirts cut back at an angle, as in *Fig 54*. The rear skirts were cut off in about 1340–50, reducing the length here to level with the back of the knees. This shortened version is referred to as the cyclas coat, and an example occurs on the effigy of Henry, Duke of Lancaster, dated 1347, on the Hastings brass at Elsyng in Norfolk: *Fig 55*.

Some time between 1350 and 1360 the shortened surcoat or cyclas began to be replaced by the jupon, another hip-length garment but much more close-fitting and often of leather, or of padded or quilted fabric, to provide extra protection for the wearer in battle or tournament. Its lower edge was usually scalloped or fringed. The jupon was also sleeveless, laced up at the sides, and in England almost invariably bore the arms of the wearer on front and back. In Europe the wearer's arms did not normally appear on the jupon. A number of jupons are illustrated in the colour plates.

That the long form of surcoat had continued to be worn alongside the cyclas and jupon is illustrated by the fact that as late as 1370 the now

elderly Sir John Chandos, whilst attempting to dismount to fight on foot, caught his spur in the skirts of his surcoat and was slain whilst thus rendered helpless. This event, and perhaps others like it, did more to end the wearing of the long surcoat than the fashion for the jupon. From this date no more examples of the surcoat appear in the sources consulted.

The jupon was in turn discarded about 1425, although isolated examples continue to occur as late as the end of that century, and for some considerable time armour was as a general rule uncovered. Some knights had their heraldic devices engraved and gilded on their plate armour, but this was a comparatively rare occurrence, governed by the cost of producing such armour.

The tabard, a short, loose-fitting garment, open at the sides and with broad, short sleeves, had been worn in isolated examples from about 1425, and coats of arms continued to be embroidered on these and on cloaks, but both these garments were more for parades and tournaments than warfare. The tabard became more popular at the end of the century and remained in general use until the middle of the 16th century, when it went out of fashion. The tabard has survived in the form of the herald's coat, embroidered with heraldic devices on front, back and sleeves. Examples of the tabard occur in the colour plates.

Ailettes
Ailettes (little wings) were small pieces of leather or sometimes parchment, usually rectangular or square but occasionally round, diamond- or even cross-shaped, which were laced to the point of each shoulder so as to stand upright above the shoulders. Some sources state that they were designed to prevent a sword cut to the side of the neck, but many of the examples studied were much too flimsy for this, and they are more likely to have been purely heraldic or ornamental, serving as extra identification 'panels' to identify the wearer from the sides. As such they were superfluous, since the curved shield and the crest already fulfilled this rôle, and the ailette was probably more of an affected fashion than anything else.

Ailettes first appear about 1270, and it is known that leather ailettes were used at a tournament

17

(40) William de Fortz: argent, a chief gules. (41) Walter de Colville: or, a fess gules. (42) Hugh de Grentmesnil: gules, a pale or. (43) Gorrevod: azure, a chevron or. (44) Guillaume de Trie: or, a bend azure. (45) Neville, Earls of Warwick, also of the Van Eyck, Van Jutphaas, Borgharts, Oultre and other Low Country families: gules, a saltire argent. (46) Teixeira and Oluja: azure, a cross argent. (47) Sir John Chandos: argent, a pile gules. (48) Bertram de Crioll: or, a canton and two chevrons gules. (49) Henry de Grey: barry of six, argent and azure.

held in Windsor Park in 1278. This surely indicates their true rôle. During the first quarter of the 14th century ailettes appear to have reached the peak of their popularity and many examples of them being worn may be seen on monuments and in documents. However, by about 1340 they seem to have declined in popularity and they do not appear much after 1350.

If a man's shield bore, say, six cinquefoils, then one cinquefoil might be painted on each ailette, but this was not always the case and in the Luterell Psalter (*circa* 1340) Sir Geoffrey Luterell is portrayed bearing his full coat of arms on his ailettes: see photograph elsewhere in this book.

51   52   53

54   55

The Livery and Maintenance System

At the end of the Hundred Years War with France (1337–1453) large numbers of professional soldiers returned to England. Many of these men were organized into private armies by the great barons, and to these armies flocked many of the yeomen and lesser gentry who needed the protection of the barons against the injustices common at that time of unrest. These yeomen and gentry entered into a contract known as Livery and Maintenance, whereby they undertook to wear

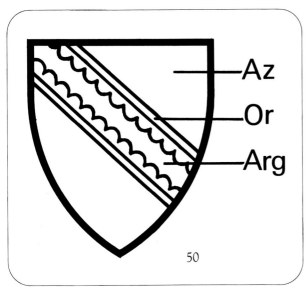

50

Az

Or

Arg

the baron's livery, i.e. a tunic in his livery colours and bearing his badge, and fight for him in time of need, while in return they would receive his protection whenever they needed it.

By 1453 the administration of justice had largely collapsed and the barons were settling their quarrels by direct action—private wars—against each other, while the rivalry between the Houses of York and Lancaster led to the Wars of the Roses (1455–85). The armies of these wars were formed mostly from the private armies of the great barons, the Livery and Maintenance men, and contract troops, that is troops raised for the Crown by contract with the king's nobles, usually a set number of men for a year's service and at an agreed wage.

Badges

The fashion for badges rose to its zenith with these large private armies of the 15th century, but badges had been used to a lesser degree in the previous century, and by royalty and a few great lords since the earliest days of heraldry. However, the badge may be said to have come into general use in the reign of Edward III, risen to its greatest

19

The seal of the great Beauchamp family, Earls of Warwick, showing shield, surcoat and trapper all bearing the family arms (Gules, a fess between six cross crosslets or) and the distinctive swan's head crest.

his banner is blazoned on the Caerlaverock Roll. Lord Talbot raised 1,800 men from the Shropshire hills for the expedition against Harfleur and the battle of Agincourt; and Edward, Duke of York and Aumerle, cousin to Henry V, raised no less than 4,000 men for the same expedition from the great Yorkist holdings of the Plantagenets.

However, by the 15th century the badge had risen to such popularity and was so necessary for the identification of troops in battle, that all commanders, no matter how small their following, began to adopt badges. Thus in the late 15th century Sir John Ferrers, who had a retinue of only two lances (one of whom was himself) and fifteen archers, had his own badge.

Because these badges were widely displayed on property, flags and liveries, they were far more widely known amongst the common people than the coats of arms of the lords, which were only displayed on a lord's person, his lance pennon and banner. In battle a lord's retainers and followers wore his badge on their clothes and rallied round a standard bearing that same badge, and consequently, unlike heraldry, the badge was a method of identification which was recognized and understood by the masses.

The badge is variously described as being worn on the sleeve or shoulder, but by the time of the Wars of the Roses it was more frequently worn on the breast.

After the Wars of the Roses a new class of nobles rose from the lower ranks to replace the great number of nobles killed in the wars. At the same time heraldry appears to have begun its decline, and almost all badges were transformed into crests. By the time of Henry VIII the crest and the badge had come to be regarded as synonymous. The decline in importance of the badge is, of course, directly linked to the creation of the standing army, which was begun in the reign of Henry VIII, for with the creation of this army the principal use of the badge—on the livery of retainers as a distinguishing mark of allegiance—came to an end.

Possibly the oldest badge is that of Geoffrey of Anjou, father of Henry II, who used the broomplant or *planta genista*—the origin of the name Plantagenet. The rose came to English royal heraldry via Eleanor of Provence, queen of

importance in the 15th century, and gone out of use in the reign of Henry VIII.

These badges were never of any fixed form, nor was there any fixed manner of usage, as with coats of arms. Also, unlike arms, they were never worn by the owner; rather they were his mark of ownership, and were therefore stamped on his belongings and worn as a sign of allegiance by his servants, dependants and retainers, who had no arms of their own and no right to bear the arms of their lord. If a lord was powerful enough to lead a party in the State, then adherents of his party might also wear his badge, and colours. (This is the origin of modern political party colours.) Such badges were generally but not always different to the charges borne on the lord's coat of arms.

Badges were originally granted by the sovereign only to those heads of great families who could field a large force of men. Such great lords normally had the right to bear a standard granted by the king at the same time, for the badge was used on the livery colours to form a standard. At the battle of Bannockburn in 1314, for example, Thomas, Lord Berkeley, had 200 retainers and was entitled to use a badge to distinguish them. Anthony Bek, Bishop of Durham, raised 80 men for the siege of Caerlaverock castle in 1300 and

Henry III, and was chosen as a badge by their heir, Edward I, who used a golden rose. His brother Edmund Crouchback, Earl of Lancaster, had a red rose and this became the badge of the Earls and Dukes of Lancaster, and of the three kings of that house—Henry IV, Henry V and Henry VI. It was also the badge of the Beaufort family, descendants of the illegitimate son of John of Gaunt, Duke of Lancaster. When Richard, Duke of York, claimed the throne in 1460 he chose a white rose as his badge, and this became the badge of his son, Edward IV, and of the Yorkist forces. Edward IV in fact placed the white rose on a sun, another Yorkist badge, and it was the confusion between this badge and the silver star of de Vere, Earl of Oxford, which cost the Lancastrians the battle of Barnet in 1471, an example of the importance of distinctive badges at that time.

Edward III had as a badge a sun bursting through clouds, *Fig 56*, and Richard II used both the *planta genista* and the sun burst, and added a personal badge of a white hart, *Fig 57*. Edward III also used an ostrich feather as a badge, *Fig 58*, which was probably derived from the arms of his wife, Philippa of Hainault. One or more ostrich feathers were used as badges by all of Edward's son, but notably by the Black Prince, who had three white feathers; and it was probably the use of this badge on a black shield and of a black surcoat to match which gave rise to the name Black Prince. From this sprang the famous Prince of Wales badge of three feathers encircled by a coronet, used by the Heir Apparent since Tudor times. Henry V used as badges the antelope,

A miniature of Sir Geoffrey Luterell taken from the Luterell Psalter, written around 1340, illustrating the placing of charges on the right side of the trapper. Compare trapper, ailette, horse crest, helmet crest and pennon with the shield and saddle arçons, where the martlets all face the dexter and the bend is not sinister.

Tudor badges on the gates of Henry VII's chapel in West-minster Abbey, including the crowned portcullis of the Beau-forts; entwined white and red roses of the Houses of York and Lancaster; crowned marguerites for Henry's mother (Lady Margaret Beaufort); and the falcon and fetterlock of the House of York; all interspersed with the fleurs-de-lys of France and lions of England.

badges are therefore standards and guidons, or monumental work in places such as Westminster Abbey. The bear and ragged staff of the Earls of Warwick, and the swan of the Earls and Dukes of Buckingham, will be familiar to many readers, but it is hoped the illustrations of badges accom-panying this section will provide examples which are new to some. *Figs 62–73* are taken from a broadsheet published in 1449, *Figs 74–79* from a manuscript of the reign of Edward IV (1461–83).

Badges occurred in European countries, al-though their use never became so widespread or so important as in England, and therefore a small selection of the more famous badges of France and Italy has been included; *Figs 80–85*.

Because they were not bound by the rules of heraldry, badges were not truly hereditary, al-though there are a number of well-known cases of the same badge being used by generation after generation. In these cases it is believed that marks of cadency were used to distinguish between the badges of father and sons. For example, Humphrey Talbot, son of John Talbot, Earl of Shrewsbury (whose badge is shown in *Fig 69*) had as a badge a talbot or hound with a mullet on its shoulder. Differencing by tincture, as with the roses of Edward I and his brother Edmund, may have been another method of denoting cadency. Sons also occasionally adopted a slightly different form of their father's badge. Other examples of differencing by cadency marks and other means may be found in the list of liveries and badges below.

Fig 59, and the swan, *Fig 61*, which were derived from his mother's family the Bohuns, and a cresset or beacon, *Fig 60*.

Royal badges became numerous under the Tudors but rarely occur after that period (1485–1603). Henry Tudor's badges included the red rose of Lancaster and the Beaufort portcullis, *Fig 62*. The Beauforts were excluded from the royal succession but, after his victory at Bosworth Field, Henry had the ban lifted by an Act of Parliament and the portcullis crowned became one of his badges as Henry VII. He also united the red and white roses into the Tudor rose when he married Elizabeth of York. The Tudor rose is found in two distinct forms; a rose divided vertically or, more commonly, a double rose with the outer petals red and the inner ones white, or vice versa.

No official records of the badges used by the king's subjects were kept until late in the reign of Henry VIII, by which time their use was rapidly declining, and therefore it is not possible to compile a complete list. Our only sources for the earlier

Liveries

Liveries were the forerunners of military uniforms, and the term livery means those distinguishing marks on the dress of individuals which marked them out as servants, retainers or followers of certain knights. In addition to this distinctive mark, the tunics of these men were usually of a

(56) **Edward III: a golden sun bursting through white (shaded) cloud.** (57) **Richard II: white hart with gold chain and crown.** (58) **Edward III: white feather with gold quill and rear faces of scroll.** (59) **Henry V: white antelope with gold crown and chain.** (60) **Henry V: beacon with red flames.** (61) **Henry V: white swan with gold crown and chain.** (62) **Henry VII: port-cullis.** (63) **John, Duke of Bedford: golden tree stump.** (64) **Humphrey, Duke of Gloucester: white duck with gold crown and chains.** (65) **de la Pole, Dukes of Suffolk: white bollard with gold strap and ring.** (66) **Mowbray, Dukes of Norfolk: a lion.** (67) **Holland, Dukes of Exeter: a beacon on a mound.**

56

57

58 *Ich dien*

59

60

61

62

63

64

65

66

67

distinctive or uniform colour or colours. Sometimes these tunics were of the principal tincture or tinctures of the arms of the leader, but livery colours were not necessarily derived from coats of arms: retainers of the house of Percy, for example, wore three stripes of russet, or and tenné with the blue lion rampant of the family arms on their shoulders as a badge. However, where the arms did provide the colours, the tincture of the field normally determined the colour of the tunic, and that of the principal charge on the field determined the colour of the edging and sometimes, on the more elaborate tunics, the lining.

Some modern writers believe that where two tinctures are listed as the colours, then the livery was divided per pale, half the coat being in each colour. There is no contemporary confirmation of this theory: in fact, in contemporary manuscripts listing colours, the liveries are frequently described as being of one colour and embroidered in the second, or divided into four stripes. Presumably tunics were only per pale, or indeed quartered, if the lord so wished it, and particularly if the field of his arms was thus divided.

The liveries of the English sovereigns during the medieval period were as follows:

The Plantagenet kings: Henry II, Richard I, John, Henry III, Edward I, and Edward II—white and red. Edward III—blue and red. Richard II—white and green.

The Lancastrian kings: Henry IV, V and VI—white and blue.

The Yorkist kings: Edward IV and Richard III—blue and murrey.

The Tudor kings: Henry VII and VIII—white and green.

A select list of liveries and badges worn by retainers of knights during the 1300–1550 period is given below. Names are listed under title, not family name; i.e. Shrewsbury, Earl of, not Talbot. Many of the knights listed had more than one badge: for space reasons only their first badge has been given:

Abergavenny, Lord of (Geo. Neville): Vt & Arg. A double staple interlaced, Arg & or.

Arundel, Earl of (Thos. FitzAlan): Az & G. A branch of oak vert, fructed or.

Audley, Sir John: Or & gu. A moor's head in profile proper, filleted round the temples, charged with a crescent for difference.

Berners, Lord (Bourchier): Or & vt. The Bourchier knot.

Brown, Sir Westyn: Gu. A lion's gamb erect and erased argent, winged sable.

Buckingham, Duke of (Edward Stafford): Gu & s. Stafford knot.

Carew, Sir William, of Devon: Four stripes s & or. A falcon collared and jessed gules, bells on neck and legs or.

Cholmondeley, Sir Richard: Gu. A helmet per pale or and argent, charged with five torteaux.

Clifford, Sir Henry: Argent. A wyvern's wings endorsed gules.

Constable, Sir Marmaduke, of Everingham, Yorks: Gules. Ancient three-masted ship headed with a dragon's head and sailed furled or, charged with a crescent sable.

Conyers, Lord of, Co. Durham: Arg. A lion passant azure.

Cornewall, Sir Thos.: Arg. A lion passant gules, ducally crowned and semé of bezants.

Curzon, Lord (Robert): Or & gu. A wolf's head erased gules.

Darcy, Thomas, Lord: Vt. An heraldic tiger argent.

Dorset, Marquess of (Thos. Grey): Arg. & pink. A unicorn ermine, armed, unguled, maned and tufted or.

Ferrers, Lord: Arg. & gu. A greyhound courant argent, ducally gorged or.

Ferrers, Sir Edward: Vt. A unicorn courant ermine, charged on the shoulder with a crescent sable.

FitzUryan, Sir Rees ap Thomas: Arg. A raven sable standing on a turf vert.

FitzUryan, Sir Griffith ap Rees: Gu & az. A quatrefoil slipped argent, leaved vert, charged with a raven sable.

Foljambe, Sir Godfrey, of Walton, Derby: Four stripes gu. & arg. A Chatloupe passant quarterly or and sable, armed or.

Grey, Lord, of Codnor: Az & arg. A badger and crown argent and or.

Gulford, Sir Henry: Arg & s. A ragged staff inflamed, charged with a mullet sable.

Gulford, Master: Four stripes wavy az & arg. A ragged staff inflamed at top and sides all proper.

Hastings, Lord: Purp & az. A bull's head erased sable, ducally gorged and armed.

Howth, Lord (The Lord Howth of Irland): Four stripes arg & gu. A wolf statant of a dark tawny, with fins along back and belly and upon hind legs 'of a water colour'.

Kent, Earl of (William Neville, Lord Fauconberg): Arg & az. A fish-hook.

Kent, Earl of (Geo. Grey): Gu. In 1475 a black ragged staff.

Kirkham, Sir John, of Blakedon, Devon: Gu. A lion's head erased argent.

Lancaster, Duke of (Henry): Arg & az. A red rose crowned.

Leicester, Earl of (Robert Dudley): Or & az. A ragged staff argent.

Massyngberd, Sir Thos. of Gunby, Lincs: Four stripes gu & or. Two arrows in saltire argent.

Norfolk, Duke of (John Mowbray): Az & tawny. A white lion.

Norfolk, Duke of (Thos. Howard): Arg & gu. A silver sallet.

Northumberland, Earl of (Henry Percy): Three stripes russet, or and tawny. A blue lion passant.

Northumberland, Duke of (John Dudley): Sable with argent and gules embroidery. A bear argent, muzzled gules, collar and chain or, supporting a ragged staff of the first.

Norton, Sir John: Gu. A greyhound's head erased in front of two wings erect all or.

Paston, Sir William, of Paston, Norfolk: Gu. A circular chain or.

Pierpoint, Sir William: Four stripes purp. & arg. A lion passant sable grasping in dexter paw a cinquefoil or.

German knight (*minnesanger*), early 14th century

A

1. Ulrich von Lichenstein, died 1275
2. Bohemian knight, second half of 14th century
3. Count Frederick von Cilli, 1415

B

1. Mathieu de Montmorency, 1360
2. Bertrand du Guesclin, died 1380
3. Jean de Créquy, *circa* 1440

C

1. John Plantagenet, Earl of Cornwall, 1316—36
2. Sir Oliver D'Ingham, died 1344
3. Sir Hugh Calveley, died 1393

D

1. Thomas Beauchamp, Earl of Warwick, 1345—1401
2. Sir John Say, 1420—78
3. Sir Edmund de Thorpe, died 1418 (?)

1. Robert de Mamines, died 1431
2. Jacopo dei Cavalli, died 1384
3. Lord of Gruthnyse, first half of 15th century

1. English herald, first half of 16th century
2. Spanish herald, *circa* 1420
3. Brandenburg pursuivant, 15th century

G

Jean de Dillon, died 1481 or 1482

Raynsforth, Sir John: Four stripes or & gu. A greyhound courant russet, plain collared or.

Richmond & Somerset, Duke of (Henry Fitzroy, natural son of Henry VIII): Three stripes arg, az & or. A lion passant guardant, ducally gorged and chained.

Roos, Lord (Geo. Manners): Az & or. A bull's head erased gules, armed, ducally gorged and chained or.

Scrope, The Lord: Arg. A Cornish chough.

Seymour, Sir John: Gu. A leopard's head or.

Shrewsbury, Earl of (John Talbot): Gu & s. A talbot dog argent.

Somerset, Duke of (John Beaufort): Bendy gu, vt & arg. An ostrich feather erect argent, the quill componé argent and azure.

Somerset, Duke of (Edward Seymour): Or & gu. A phoenix.

Stourton, Lord of, in Wiltshire: Arg & s. A gold sledge.

Suffolk, Duke of (William de la Pole): Az & or. A bollard argent with chain or.

Tyler, Sir William: Four stripes arg & az. A crescent, and issuant therefrom a cross patée fitche gules.

Vaughan, Sir Hugh, of Lytylton: Four stripes or & vt. A fishhead erased and erect or, 'ingullant' of a spear's head argent.

Vernon, Sir Henry: Arg & or. A fret sable.

Warwick, Earl of Salisbury and (Richard Nevill): Gu (1458). White ragged staff.

Willoughby, Lord: Arg & gu. A moor's head full faced, the tongue hanging out.

Wiltshire: Earl of (Henry): S & gu. A Stafford knot charged with a crescent gules for difference.

Zouche, John, son and heir of Lord Zouche: S & purp. On the branch of a tree or, sprouting vert, an eagle rising argent, gorged with a label of three points.

Zouche, John, of Codnor: Gu & vt. On the stump of a tree or, branching vert, a falcon, wings elevated argent, charged on the breast with a crescent gules. (Also the badger and crown argent and or of Lord Grey of Codnor.)

The Wars of the Roses virtually extinguished the Livery and Maintenance system—the greater part of the baronage was dead and the whole country was sick of war—and under the strong rule of Henry Tudor (1485–1509) such private armies were at last made illegal. Nevertheless the system of raising an army in time of need by calling on nobles to supply men was retained, and so therefore were many of the individual liveries of these lords. Under this contract system, nobles were obliged to supply men by the hundred, depending on their status: gentlemen or ordinary knights had to supply two men, and a squire one man.

As early as 1345 Parliament had enacted that troops raised for the French wars were to be dressed in a uniform manner, and eleven years later, at the battle of Poitiers, the army of the Black Prince did in fact wear a uniform of green and white—the livery colours adopted by the next king (Richard II) and subsequently used by Henry VII and Henry VIII. By the late 14th century the red cross of St George on a white background, first adopted for the crusades, was the recognized badge of the English soldier, worn either as a coat or as a distinctive part of a coat, and by the time of Agincourt Henry V had ordained that 'every man, of what estate or condition, that be of our partie, beare a bande of Seinte George sufficient large' upon his clothes (on the chest and back). Nobles, bannerets and knights also wore their jupons bearing the family arms, and there are many references to them putting these on at the king's or other leaders' command just before a battle was joined, and taking them off immediately after the battle. Some form of 'uniform' was obviously desirable in the battles now being fought.

By 1501 the 300-strong Yeomen of the Guard (archers of the King's Bodyguard, formed in 1485 by Henry Tudor) were dressed in the Tudor livery colours of white and green in vertical stripes, embroidered on chest and back with a red rose within a vine wreath. This coat would have been the ordinary horseman's coat of the period, probably sleeveless and close fitting but with a wide skirt. Under Henry VIII (1509–47) these Yeomen still wore white and green for the 1514 campaign in France, but are shown to have worn at the Field of the Cloth of Gold in 1520 a red tunic with black bars at the edges and on the arms, with the rose surmounted by a crown in gold on chest and back. Hose and doublets were white. (The Field of the Cloth of Gold painting was finished *circa* 1538 and in fact the Tudor rose remained uncrowned until 1527 or possibly later.) Red gradually replaced the white and green as dress uniform for ceremonial occasions, but the white and green tunics persisted for everyday use until about 1530.

Similarly the various companies of the English army of the 16th century and the shire and city levies (or trained bands) now wore some form of 'uniform', basically still their lord's (or captain's—often the same thing) livery colours and badge. Thus in 1554 the men of the Earl of Pembroke wore blue coats with a green dragon badge; the men-at-arms of the Marquess of Winchester had embroidered coats of red and white in about 1570; while those of the Earl of Suffolk in 1597 had blue coats faced with sea-green taffeta, with

68

69

70

71

72

73

74

75

76

77

78

79

feathers of the same colours and 'many chains of gold'. Even in the early 17th century such livery uniforms persisted: in 1603 the men of the Earl of Norwich wore blue livery coats with white doublets, hats and feathers, and those of the Earl of Nottingham in 1605 had cloaks of orange-tawny, edged with silver and blue lace. This earl's trumpeters wore orange damask clothing, with cloaks of the same colour.

In the trained bands some attempt was also made to wear a distinguishing dress in battle. In 1513 the men of Canterbury wore the chough, from the city's coat of arms, on their chest and back. In 1522 the men of Shrewsbury were issued with coats bearing leopards' heads. The soldiers raised by the City of London in 1539 had white coats bearing the arms of the city on front and back, and in 1542 the cavalry raised by Coventry had an elephant badge on their coats. The men of Norwich in 1543 wore a blue coat edged and decorated with red and, for the first time on record, their hose was also regulated: all red for the right leg, blue with a broad red stripe for the left leg.

In 1544 Henry VIII is portrayed landing in France wearing over his armour a tunic of white and gold with a red cross in the centre, and apparently the traditional red cross of St George on a white background was now usually worn together with the company's badge, either with the badge set somewhere on a white tunic bearing the red cross, or the red cross on a white background set on part of the company's coat. However, in 1556 the men of Reading were still wearing blue coats with red crosses, their hose being in various colours, so true 'national' uniform does not appear to have been adopted at this date. In fact, although all men of each county now wore one distinctive livery, the various counties were still dressed in different 'uniforms', and some of the counties even went so far as to vary that 'uniform' from year to year.

Red and blue were the predominant colours of these county liveries—red was also a usual colour for English military headgear in the 16th century —and these two colours remained the most popular in the latter half of the century.

All these examples illustrate early attempts to identify troops in battle by means of uniform dress. However, at this stage only the tunic or livery was normally affected; hats and hose of various hues were worn by men within the same companies, and there was not yet any such thing as a universal uniform or a national colour for coats.

Crests

Some forms of helmet crest seem to have come into use towards the end of the 12th century and beginning of the 13th century, but it is not until the beginning of the 14th century that heraldic crests began to come into general use and take on a three-dimensional form. From this date on crests are often referred to as 'true' crests, in that they are free-standing, three-dimensional constructions.

These 'true' crests were rather splendid, often fantastic objects, made of a fairly lightweight material such as moulded leather, parchment, whalebone, beaten copper sheet, plumes and feathers, canvas stretched over a wicker frame, thin wood, or papier mâché. Leather was probably the most prevalent, in the form of *cuir bouilli*, that is leather soaked in hot wax and bent to shape while still hot. This had the advantages of being light yet strong, and could be shaped easily. (*Cuir bouilli* was also used to cover shields, with heraldic charges embossed upon it, and for making a form of body and horse armour.)

The feathers of cockerels, swans and peacocks were also used extensively. They were usually arranged as a panache, particularly in the earlier crests, that is rising in tiers to a point, as in the crests of Edmund Mortimer (1372), *Fig 86*, Sir Edward Thorpe (1418), *Fig 87*, and John, Lord Scrope, *Fig 88*; or as a plume, in which only one or two tiers were employed, as in the crest of the Earl of Hereford in 1301, *Fig 89*. The panache sometimes spread outwards instead of rising to a point, as in the crest of Sir Simon de Felbrigge, *Fig 90*, and that of John, King of Bohemia, *Fig 91*. On occasions feathers were also displayed in a cluster, as in the brass to Sir Thomas de St Quintin (1420),

(68) de Vere, Earls of Oxford. (69) Talbot, Earls of Shrewsbury. (70) Neville, Earls of Warwick. (71) FitzAlan, Earls of Arundel. (72) Courtenay, Earls of Devon. (73) Richard, Duke of York: a golden fetterlock. (74) Scales, Earl Rivers. (75) Earls of Douglas. (76) Lord Scrope of Bolton. (77) Lord Grey of Codnor. (78) Sir Ralph Hastings. (79) Sir John Astley.

80   81   82

83   84   85

(80) **The ermine of the Dukes of Brittany.** (81) **The porcupine of the House of Orleans.** (82) **The winged hart of the House of Bourbon.** (83) **The salamander of the House of Angoulême.** (84) **The serpent and child of the Dukes of Milan.** (85) **The knot of the House of Savoy.**

Fig 92. The feathers were occasionally coloured in the principal tinctures of the arms, as in the crest of the Comte de Namur, *Fig 93, circa* 1295, whose arms were Or, a lion rampant sable, armed, crowned and langued gules, overall a bend gules.

Horns were another popular form of crest in Germany and to a lesser extent in England: *Figs 94* and *95* show two German examples, *Fig 96* the crest of Sir John Plessis (13th century). In the earlier crests these horns were simply curved and pointed—in their natural form—but in the later, more elaborate crests they are sometimes recurved (as *Fig 95*) and have an opening into which are sometimes inserted tufts or plumes of feathers. These horns are usually painted in the tinctures of the shield.

The human figure is another favourite crest in German heraldry, usually shown half-length and sometimes with the arms replaced by horns, as in *Fig 97*, the crest of the Count of Montbeliard. The hat is another common crest in German heraldry, *Fig 98*, the crest of the 14th-century knight, Casteln.

The heads of heraldic beasts such as lions, boars, hounds, and of heraldic birds such as eagles, swans and cockerels, accounted for many of the other crests. In some cases these consisted of a repetition of a charge in the wearer's arms, but often the charges in arms did not lend themselves to use in crests, and consequently it became

The bronze effigy of Georg Truchsess von Waldburg (died 1467) in St Peter's Church, Bad Waldsee in Württemberg, showing a crest of green peacock's feathers in a panache and a second crest of a fir tree, as well as his banner and shield, bearing his arms, Or, three lions sable. The arms of the princes zu Waldburg had originally been Azure, three pine cones or, and this is probably the origin of the second crest.

28

common practice for many knights to use a crest which was in no way linked with their arms.

Apart from Richard I, who is shown wearing a fan-shaped crest on his Great Seal of 1194, no English monarch wore a crest until Edward III, who wore a lion on a chapeau, *Fig 99*. He also had a 'personal' crest of an eagle. The crest of Henry V in Westminster Abbey is an uncrowned lion on a chapeau, *Fig 100*, the lion being passant: that of Richard II is an uncrowned lion, passant guardant, *Fig 101*. All other English kings have used a crowned lion, passant guardant, as in *Fig 99*. In Tudor times a crown was substituted for the chapeau, and this has been the English royal crest ever since. All other members of the royal family in England also bore a lion crest, with the single exception of Thomas, Earl of Lancaster, who wore a wyvern, *Fig 102*, *circa* 1347. This, combined with Edward III's personal crest, is interesting in that amongst English chivalry in particular it is known that the crest was considered a personal rather than a hereditary device, and was therefore subject to change, different members of the same family normally using different crests.

Crests were worn primarily at the tournament, or other pageants and parades, and by the 14th century were not designed for the battlefield. It is believed that by this date the 'true' crest may have been a mark of special dignity, possibly only awarded to persons of rank and entitling them to take part in tournaments. Certainly in the 15th century the use of crests was almost entirely linked to tournaments, and as the armour and equipment had by this date become so elaborate and costly, only the wealthy could afford to participate. The jousting score-sheets kept by the English heralds of the time confirm this, the names of the same men recurring time after time. This situation had probably existed since the late 14th century. The elaborate and flamboyant crests worn by knights for the tournament were therefore heraldic status symbols which indicated both that the wearer was of tournament rank and that he could afford to participate! This explains why so few of the lesser gentry in England had crests before 1530, and it is mainly as crests that the more fabulous and chimerical creatures of heraldry appear.

In Germany and the Low Countries crests were regarded by the heralds as being of great importance from an early date (certainly by the early 13th century) and the crests used in these countries in the 14th and 15th centuries were also directly linked to the tournament and were often extremely tall and fanciful as a result. See *Figs 95, 103* and *104; 103* being the crest of the lord of Badenweiler in Baden, and *104* of the knight Aeschach.

Crests were seldom used in France, Italy, Spain and Portugal, and in Spain especially examples of crests are almost unknown even amongst the greatest families. A rare example of an Italian crest is given in *Fig 105*, that of Mastino II (died 1351) of the della Scala family, from the tomb in Verona. Examples of French crests are also rare, and those which do survive usually belong to the highest in the land, for example *Fig 106*, crest of the King of France in the 14th century; *Fig 107*, that of the Duc de Bourgogne *circa* 1295; *Fig 108*, that of Philip IV, King of France 1285–1314; and *Fig 109*, the crest of Bertrand du Guesclin. (See also *Fig 93*, the crest of the Comte de Namur *circa* 1295.)

In Poland all nobles wore the same type of crest, three ostrich feathers, irrespective of family arms.

The Scarf

The scarf or *contoise* was a piece of cloth, possibly originating from a lady's favour or in imitation of the turban, which presumably had some practical purpose, such as protection from the weather, although it is hard to see exactly what its value would have been. Illustrations of the scarf show it to have been of various lengths (see *Figs 94* and *102*), sometimes reaching only to the neck, other times capable of reaching halfway down the back. In some examples it is fastened to the top of the helmet, in others it emerges from beneath the edge at the rear of the helmet.

Although the scarf is believed to have originated during the crusades period, it does not appear frequently in illustrations until the early 14th century, and it was replaced soon after this date by the wreath and mantling described over.

See body of text for identifications; note details: (86) Blue feathers. (87) Peacock's feathers. (93) A semé of gold hearts on the mantling. (96) Peacock's feathers. (97) Gold hair, crown and 'horns', with red gown as mantling.

86

87

88

89

90

91

92

93

94

95

96

97

A horse armour, known as the Burgundian bard, probably Flemish, *circa* 1510. This bard is heavily embossed with the emblems of the Order of the Golden Fleece and reflects the extravagant fashion of having coats of arms engraved and gilded on armour after jupons had gone out of fashion.

The Wreath

The wreath developed from the scarf and appeared by the mid-14th century. Unlike the scarf, which had served a useful purpose, the wreath was purely ornamental. It was made of two skeins of silk or other material, in the tinctures of the field and principal charge of the wearer's arms, twisted together to form a ring. The crest was laced or bolted to the helmet and the wreath was attached to the base of the crest to conceal this joint. Examples of the wreath appear in *Figs 107* and *109*.

A cap or chapeau, an ancient cap of dignity worn by dukes and made of scarlet fur with a turn-up of ermine, was worn instead of a wreath by the high ranking nobles. It is illustrated in the crests of the kings of England, *Figs 99, 100* and *101*. After the reign of Edward III a coronet was worn by dukes, princes and the king.

In a few examples a wreath is used as a 'crest', or crest-wreath, as *Fig 110*, that of Lord Willoughby d'Eresby, 1409. See also the cluster of feathers held by a brooch on the helmet of Sir Thomas de St Quintin, *Fig 92*.

Mantling

The mantling was merely a larger version of the scarf, originally designed to protect the helmet and its wearer from the elements. It was mainly a form of decoration, however, and was probably only used for the tournament. The mantling was in the principal colour of the wearer's arms, its underside the colour of the principal metal or fur.

It was sometimes decorated with charges from the arms, or the wearer's badge. For example, John D'Aubynge, *circa* 1345, had a semé of mullets on his mantling (*Fig 111*); George, Duke of Clarence, a semé of the white roses of York; Henry Bourchier, Earl of Essex (died 1485), billety, with the lining having a semé of water budgets. In some cases the material of the crest, especially if that material was a textile or feathers, was continued downwards to form the mantling, as in the crests of the German knights Badenweiler (*Fig 103*), Chur (*Fig 112*), Hevtler (*Fig 113*), and in Sir Simon de Felbrigge's ermine panache (*Fig 90*). The black boar's head crest of Sir Ralph Basset (*Fig 114*) also continues into a sable mantling.

Horse Trappers

While all horse trappers, or caparisons, are divided into two halves which meet at the saddle, they differ in the forward half, some completely covering the horse's head, others ending behind its ears, and still others ending at the shoulders to leave neck and head free. In the early examples the trappers are of cloth, full and loose, and reach to the fetlocks: some of these have a dagged edge, though this is not common.

By the mid-15th century the trapper had begun to be influenced by the general increase in the use of plate armour, but because the cost and weight of such armour was prohibitive, leather armour was commonly used for horses. This was painted with the rider's arms in the same way as the now purely ornamental cloth trapper. The great lords who did use plate on their horses for the tournament covered these bards with richly embroidered cloth trappers, secured in place by laces.

The basic colour of a caparison was normally the principal tincture of the rider's arms, with the principal charge or charges repeated on each side of each half of the trapper. Livery colours were sometimes used instead of the tinctures of the and green velvet, embroidered with golden swans had no connection at all with the rider's arms— particularly in Germany. It is interesting to note in this context that when the Duke of Hereford (later Henry IV), rode to fight a duel (a duel stopped by Richard II) with the Duke of Norfolk

near Coventry, his horse wore a trapper of blue and green velvet, embroidered with golden swans and antelopes, and that when Henry V's body was returned to England after his death in France, the horses conveying the body wore trappers of blue and green velvet, embroidered with antelopes.

The actual designs on trappers needs a little clarification. A knight bearing, for example, Gules, three water budgets argent (the arms of William, Lord Ros, temp. Edward I) would probably have a red trapper with three white water budgets on each side of the rear half, and three more water budgets on each side of the front half. However, he might choose to use only one water budget on each side of each half, or to employ his entire coat of arms on a shield as a device, that shield being perhaps repeated three times on each side of each half of the trapper, or as a single device on each side of each half.

There is also the problem of which side is dexter, which sinister, when applied to the two sides of a horse. From the examples studied it would seem that the horse's head was regarded as being on the dexter side; and therefore on the left-hand side, or shielded side as we view it, the trapper bore the arms exactly as they appeared on the shield. On the other side of the trapper, the charges of the coat of arms were reversed, so that they still faced towards the horse's head. A study of the photograph of Sir Geoffrey Luterell mounted, on page 21, should make this point clear, for in this example the right-hand side of the horse is shown and Sir Geoffrey's trapper, crest and ailettes all bear the charges of his arms reversed.

The Plates

A: German knight (minnesanger), early 14th century
This figure is taken from the famous Manesse Codex at Heidelberg, compiled at the beginning of the 14th century. The *minnesanger* was the approximate equivalent of the French *troubadour* and usually came from the lower nobility. In this example he and his horse are decked in the full panoply of a medieval knight: horse trapper, surcoat, crest, lance banner, and shield bearing

98   99   100

101   102   103

104   105   106

107   108   109

his coat of arms. It was normal practice for the surcoat, crest and trapper to be either in the colours of the arms or to bear the charges shown on those arms, but, as may be seen from this illustration, this was by no means a hard and fast rule. The symbol on the surcoat is believed to be a stylized letter 'A', for *Amor*, and in the original manuscript this *minnesanger* is shown receiving his helm from the lady he is wooing.

B1 : *Ulrich von Lichenstein, died 1275*

As in the preceding plate, this figure is taken from the Manesse Codex. Ulrich von Lichenstein was a Styrian poet who died *circa* 1275, but the armour and crest he wears are typical of those worn by the lesser German knights in the first half of the 14th century. His surcoat is unrelated to his arms, but does bear his coat of arms on a shield. His horse trapper was of the same green material and bore three shields with his arms on each side of the front and rear halves.

Both this and the figure in Plate A are dressed as if for the tourney, and von Lichenstein is in fact armed with a tourney lance with three-pointed (coronel) head.

B2 : *Bohemian knight, second half of 14th century*

By this date the close-fitting jupon had replaced the surcoat. Unlike the surcoat, the jupon rarely bore the wearer's arms (except in England) and in this example the knight is portrayed with only a shield bearing arms (of the Holy Roman Empire) and holding a lance with a pennon bearing the Hungarian colours. The figure is based on an illustration in a Bohemian chess book of 1350–1400.

B3 : *Count Frederick von Cilli, 1415*

Based on a contemporary illustration which shows the count outside the walls of Coutances on 20 March 1415, waiting to joust with Duke Frederick of Austria. His jousting shield bears the arms of the von Cilli family and the crest is the one used by all members of that family. His trapper was of the

same colour as his helmet mantling, and each half bore on each side a shield displaying his arms.

C1 : *Mathieu de Montmorency, 1360*

This illustration of the Chevalier Mathieu de Montmorency is based on the effigy on his tomb at Tavergny in France. There is no heraldry on the jupon and he would have been identified in battle solely by his shield and lance pennon. No helmet is shown on the tomb effigy, but it would probably have been of the general type shown on Plate D3. Note the difference of a three-pointed label over the arms, indicating this particular warrior was a cadet of the great Montmorency family.

C2 : *Bertrand du Guesclin, died 1380*

One of France's greatest military leaders during the Hundred Years War, du Guesclin was made Constable of France in October 1370, thus placing even the royal princes under his command. In the contemporary print upon which this illustration is based, du Guesclin carries a shield bearing a lion and with the arms of France (modern) in chief, but we have shown his personal arms. It is worth pointing out that his arms are not repeated on his jupon, nor does he wear an elaborate crest. (His tourney crest is shown in *Fig 109*.) Like the figures shown in B2 and C1, du Guesclin is dressed for battle: it was only at the tournament that elaborate jupons, crests and trappers were used.

C3 : *Jean de Créquy, circa 1440*

Jean, *Seigneur* de Créquy, was ambassador to Spain and France for the Duke of Burgundy and is shown here dressed for the tourney with elaborate crest and tabard. The charge on his arms is a stylized wild cherry tree, in French *créquier*, and his arms are therefore of the type known as canting arms. Jean de Créquy was a knight of the Order of the Golden Fleece (instituted in 1429 by Philip the Good, Duke of Burgundy) and this illustration is based on an original in the 15th-century *Armorial of the Knights of the Golden Fleece*. His father Jacques de Créquy was taken prisoner and put to death at the battle of Agincourt.

D1 : *John Plantagenet, Earl of Cornwall, 1316–36*

John Plantagenet bears the arms of England dif-

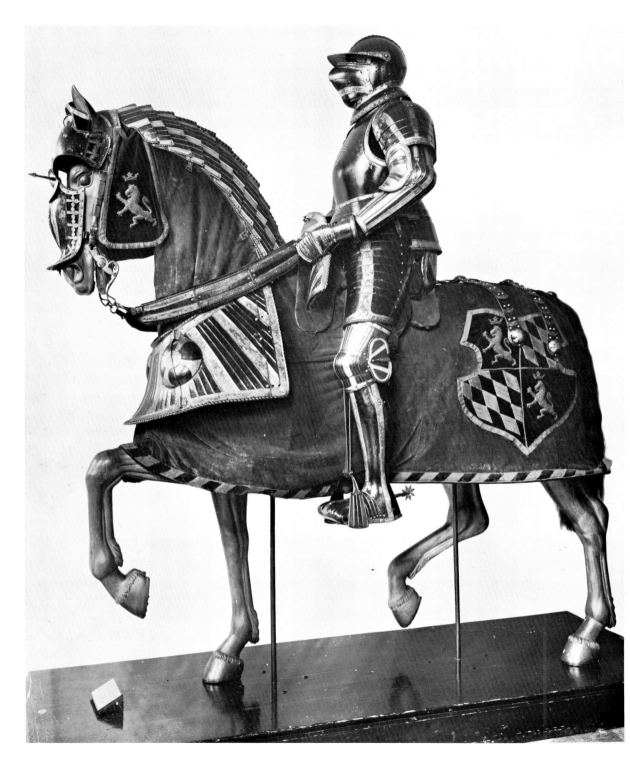

A horse armour made for Otto Heinrich, Count Palatine of the Rhine, between 1532–36. The arms of the Palatinate and Bavaria appear on the rear half of the bard and are repeated on a small shield on the front of the chanfron. The lion appears again at the side of the head, while the tinctures of the arms of the Palatinate are employed on the border of the bard.

ferenced with a bordure of France—a combination of the arms of his father, Edward II, and mother, Queen Isabel of France. He was created Earl of Cornwall in 1328, was regent for Edward III while that king was in France (1329–31) and commanded the English army in Scotland. His arms are repeated on his cyclas. This figure is based on the effigy in Westminster Abbey.

D2: Sir Oliver D'Ingham, died 1344

Sir Oliver had a distinguished career in the reigns of Edward II and Edward III, and was Seneschal of Aquitaine in 1325–26 and 1333–43. He gained a decisive victory over the French at Bordeaux in 1340. The early arms of the Ingham family appear to have had a white field and the party field shown here was probably derived from the arms of Bigod, Earls of Norfolk, where the Ingham lands lay. The illustration is based on the effigy in Ingham Church, though the arms on the cyclas are after Stothard (1811). The helmet with crest at the head of the monument is now mutilated beyond recognition, but John Weever, writing in 1613, stated that the crest was an owl on a thorn bush.

D3: Sir Hugh Calveley, died 1393

Sir Hugh was one of the most famous captains of the free companies in the Hundred Years War. He served in Spain with Henry of Trastamare in 1366, and later joined the army of the Black Prince. He was appointed deputy of Calais in 1377, and in 1380 took part in the unsuccessful expedition to France led by the Duke of Gloucester. He was governor of the Channel Isles, 1376–88.

He is shown in a jupon bearing his canting arms and wearing his tourney helm with crest of a calf's head. The arms are an early example in English heraldry of the use of two differently coloured charges on one field. This illustration is based on the effigy in Bunbury Church, Cheshire.

E1: Thomas Beauchamp, Earl of Warwick, 1345–1401

Thomas Beauchamp was a warrior and military governor throughout the reign of Edward III, but in the following reign he joined various plots against the king and was imprisoned in the Tower. He was released and had his honours restored on the accession of Henry IV. His jupon bears the arms of the Beauchamps, while the plates at his elbows, on the sword-belt and scabbard are decorated with the ragged staff badge of Warwick. Other branches of the family used the same colours but replaced the crosses crosslet with different charges. The figure is based on the brass at St Mary's Church, Warwick.

E2: Sir John Say, 1420–78

Sir John was probably a son of John Say of Podington in Bedfordshire, and possibly a kinsman of Lord Saye and Sele. Although brought up a Lancastrian, he became a Yorkist in 1460 and on his tomb brass wears round his neck a Yorkist collar of alternate suns and roses. He was a prominent figure in Parliament and was knighted in 1465. His tabard bears his arms, which are repeated on each sleeve. The figure is based on a brass made during his lifetime (in 1473) and which is in Broxbourne Church, Hertfordshire.

E3: Sir Edmund de Thorpe, died 1418 (?)

Sir Edmund was a prominent soldier in the wars of Henry V, and is believed to have been killed at the siege of Louviers in 1418. His jupon bears the arms of Thorpe (Azure, three crescents argent) quartered with those of his mother, daughter and heiress of Robert Baynard (Sable, a fess between two chevrons or). He is shown wearing his tourney helmet with crest, this and other information shown here being taken from his effigy in Ashwellthorpe Church, Norfolk.

F1: Robert de Mamines, died 1431

Robert de Mamines was a leading Flemish soldier who followed Jean 'Sans Peur', father of Philip III. He was killed at Liège in 1431. He appears here attired for the tourney, in blazoned tabard and highly decorative crested helmet, as illustrated in the *Armorial of the Knights of the Golden Fleece*. He was created a knight of this Order in 1430 at the siege of Melun.

F2: Jacopo dei Cavalli, died 1384

Based on an effigy in SS Giovanni e Paolo, Venice, this is another example of canting arms. Note the knight's arms do not appear on his jupon.

F3: Lord of Gruthuyse, first half of 15th century

This Flemish knight is thus portrayed in the famous 15th-century *Livre des Tournois*. The same manuscript shows this lord's herald, wearing a tabard bearing his lord's arms, and his trumpeter, whose trumpet has a banner bearing the same arms. The family name is also spelt Groothuys and Gruthuse in contemporary sources, and in the *Armorial of the Knights of the Golden Fleece* (compiled between 1430 and 1440) is listed a Monsieur de Grutusse, who bears these same arms but with the quarters reversed. A Gruthuse served in the army of the Duke of Burgundy in 1417.

G1: English herald, first half of 16th century

This figure is taken from a parade of English officers of arms, illustrated in a tourney book of the time of Henry VIII. The pursuivants had a similar tabard but wore it askew, that is with the short arm panels over chest and back, and the longer panels over their arms.

G2: Spanish herald, circa 1420

The Sicily herald illustrated here served the king of Aragon, to whom Sicily then belonged, around 1420. He wears the arms of Sicily and Aragon. This particular herald, Jean Courteois, was responsible for the most authoritative written record of the rights and duties of a herald.

(110) **Lord Willoughby D'Eresby.** (111) **John D'Aubynge.** (112) **14th-century German knight named Chur: red jester's cap with gold edge and white balls.** (113) **14-century German knight named Hevtler: red edging to mantling, red beak and embattled upper half to spinal crest.** (114) **Sir Ralph Basset, Knight of the Garter 1368–90: gold tusks and coronet.** (115) **de Montacute, Earls of Salisbury, 1337–44, 1397–1400: gold griffin and coronet.** (116) **Humphrey, Earl of Stafford, Knight of the Garter, 1429: white swan, red beak, gold coronet.** (117) **The Burgrave of Nuremburg: the mantling was probably black.** (118) **14th-century knight from Basle named Schaler: white lozengy on red.** (119) **Nicholas de Borssele, 15th-century French knight.** (120) **Charles, Comte de Valois, *circa* 1295.** (121) **14th-century German knight named Bretsla: green peacock's feathers with red eyes on yellow, yellow background to eagle, white crescent, red mantling edged yellow.**

G3: Brandenburg pursuivant, 15th century

German pursuivants wore their tabards in the same fashion as the heralds. The one illustrated here was pursuivant of the Elector Frederick II of Brandenburg (1413–71). His official title was *Burggraf*, because his master, as a Hohenzollern, was also the *burgrave* of Nuremburg.

H: Jean de Dillon, died 1481 or 1482

Jean de Dillon was the king of France's representative in Arras, and this portrait of him is based on a *mille-fleur* tapestry made there, probably in 1477. Note that by this late date the knight does

A German sallet for a light horseman, *circa* 1490, painted with heraldic charges. In the early days of heraldry 'crests' were often painted on helmets before the true crest developed: this example suggests 'crests' for the lower nobility may have come full circle by the late 15th century.

110

111

112

113

114

115

116

117

118

119

120

121

39

not wear any heraldic devices on his person and, as shields were no longer carried in battle, he could only be identified by his lance pennon or banner. Thus from *circa* 1450 at the latest the flag became the sole means of identifying individual lords on the field of battle, and the military rôle of heraldry had come to an end, to be superseded by the age of the military flag, at least until the reintroduction of heraldic symbols in the form of formation signs in the First World War.

Notes sur les planches en couleur

A Il n'arrivait pas toujours que le surcot, le cimier et le harnachement du cheval soient aux couleurs des armoiries et portent les mêmes emblèmes. On pense que le surcot porte ici la lettre 'A' stylisée pour Amor. Nous avons tiré ce cavalier du Manuscrit Manesse à Heidelberg.

B1 Comme dans le cas de l'illustration A, le personnage tiré du Manuscrit Manesse est habillé pour le tournoi et tient à la main une lance à trois pointes appelée 'coronel'. Le harnachement des chevaux de von Lichtenstein était vert et orné de trois écussons à ses armoiries de chaque côté des moitiés avant et arrière. **B2** Extraite d'un Livre d'Echecs bohémien datant de la fin du 14ème siècle, cette illustration montre le jupon cintré qui remplaçait alors le surcot plus lâche. Le bouclier porte les armoiries du Saint Empire Romain et la flamme de lance est aux couleurs hongroises. **B3** La couronne était portée par tous les membres de cette famille et le bouclier de joute porte les armoiries de la famille von Cilli.

C1 Illustration basée sur l'effigie d'une tombe à Tavergny en France. Le casque n'est pas illustré mais il ressemblerait probablement à celui de l'illustration D3. **C2** Le Grand Connétable de France porte un bouclier à ses propres armoiries; l'apparence généralement simple de ce costume est caractéristique de la tenue de combat plutôt que de la tenue d'apparat de tournoi. **C3** Tenue de tournoi élaborée. Ses armoiries ont un 'cerisier sauvage' stylisé — en français créquier — une contrepèterie sur le nom.

D1 Extrait d'une effigie de l'Abbaye de Westminster. Ce chevalier porte les armes d'Angleterre avec en bordure les armes de France, un mélange des armoiries de son père Edouard II et de celles de sa mère Isabelle de France. **D2** Le Sénéchal d'Aquitaine au début du 14ème siècle, Sir Oliver, remporta une grande victoire sur les français à Bordeaux en 1340. Ses armoiries semblent être dérivées de celles de la Famille Bigod, Comtes de Norfolk, Comté dans lequel se trouvaient ses terres. **D3** Extrait de l'effigie d'une tombe. Sir Hugh était un célèbre chef de mercenaires, il se battit pour le Prince Noir et ses armoiries sont un jeu de mots sur son nom en anglais.

E1 Jupon aux armoiries de la Famille Beauchamp et les plaquettes aux coudes, ceinturon et fourreau portent l'écusson de Warwick au motif 'ragged staff'. **E2** Sir John naquit dans l'esprit de la Maison de Lancastre mais devait se rallier à celle de York en 1460. Il porte ici ses armoiries sur son tabard et elles sont reprises sur les manches. **E3** Extrait de l'effigie d'une tombe. Casque de tournoi avec cimier. Sir Edmund fut un grand soldat de Henri V tué à Louviers en 1418.

F1 Tiré des documents de l'Ordre de la Toison d'Or auquel le Chevalier flamand de Mamines fut admis en 1430 au siège de Melun. Il porte ici une tenue de tournoi très ornée. **F2** Extrait de l'effigie d'une tombe à Venise; remarquer que le jupon ne porte pas d'armoiries. **F3** Un chevalier flamand; nous avons tiré cette illustration du Livre des Tournois du 15ème siècle.

G1 Tiré d'un Livre des Tournois du règne de Henri VIII d'Angleterre. **G2** Le Chevalier de Sicile servant le Roi d'Aragon et portant les armes de Sicile et d'Aragon. **G3** Ce chevalier est le *Burggraf* de l'Electeur de Brandebourg.

H Jean de Dillon illustré d'après une tapisserie faite à Arras où il était le représentant du Roi de France vers 1477. L'armure n'est recouverte d'aucun vêtement héraldique et du fait qu'à cette époque on portait rarement de bouclier pendant les batailles, la bannière devint le principal signe d'identité.

Farbtafeln

A Es kam nicht immer vor, dass Wappenrock, Helmbusch und Pferdeschmuck in der eigentlichen Wappenfarbe ausgeführt war und die gleichen Sinnbilder trugen. Vermutlich ist der Symbol auf dem Wappenrock ein stilisiertes 'A', d.h. Amor. Diese Figur ist von dem Manesse Codex zu Heidelberg entnommen worden.

B1 Von dem Manesse Codex entnommen ist auch diese Figur, die—wie jene in A—für Ritterturnier angezogen ist und in der Hand eine Lanze mit dreifacher Spitze oder 'coronel' hält. Von Lichtensteins Pferdeschmuck war in grün ausgeführt und war auf jeder Seite mit drei Wappenschildern sowohl den Hinter- als auf den Vorderteilen geschmückt. **B2** Von einem böhmischen Schachbuch des späten 14. Jahrhunderts, stellt diese Farbtafel das enganliegende *jupon* dar, das mittlerweile den loser hängenden Wappenrock ersetzt hatte. Auf dem Schilde steht das Wappen des Heiligen Römischen Reichs und das Lanzenfähnchen ist in ungarischen Wappenfarben ausgeführt. **B3** Dieser Helmbusch wurde von allen Mitgliedern dieser Familie getragen; der Turnierschild trägt das Wappen der Familie von Cilli.

C1 Nach einem Grabbildnis zu Taverny in Frankreich abgebildet. Kein Helm wird vorgezeigt, jedoch wäre er dem in D3 abgebildeten Helme ähnlich gewesen sein. **C2** Hier trägt der Grosse Konnetabel von Frankreich, einen Schild worauf sein persönliches Wappen aufgetragen ist; in der allgemeinen Einfachheit seines Ansehens sieht man eher die typische Schlachtaustrüstung als Turnierstaat. **C3** Ausgearbeitete Turnierausrüstung. Das Wappen enthält einen stilisierten 'Wildkirschbaum' auf französisch—*créquier*—ein Wortspiel über seinem Namen.

D1 Von einem Bildnis zu Westminster Abbey entnommen. Er trägt das Wappen von England mit einer *bordure* aus dem Wappen von Frankreich, eine Zusammenstellung des Wappens seines Vaters, König Edward II, und seiner Mutter, die Königin Isabelle von Frankreich. **D2** Hausmeier von Aquitaine im frühen 14. Jahrhundert, hat Sir Oliver die Franzosen bedeutsam im Jahre 1340 bei Bordeaux besiegt. Scheinbar ist sein Wappen von dem der Familie Bigod, die Grafen von Norfolk, abstammig; seine Ländereien befanden sich in dieser Grafschaft. **D3** Nach einem Grabbildnis abgebildet: Sir Hugh war ein bekannter Söldnerführer, der unter Kommando des Schwarzen Prinzen gekämpft hat. Sein Wappen stellt ein Wortspiel über seinem englischen Namen dar.

E1 Auf dem *jupon* befindet sich das Wappen der Familie Beauchamp und die kleinen Platten an den Ellenbogen und am Gürtel sind mit dem 'gezackten Stabe' von Warwick geschmückt. **E2** Gebürtig gehörte Sir John zur Partei von Lancaster, ist aber im Jahre 1460 zur Partei von York übergegangen. Hier trägt er sein Wappen auf einem *tabard* (Heroldsrock) und wiederholt auf beiden Ärmel. **E3** Nach einem Grabbildnis abgebildet. Sir Edmund trägt einen Turnierhelm mit Helmbusch. Ein berühmter Soldat unter Henry V, ist er im Jahre 1418 zu Louviers gefallen.

F1 Aus den Urkunden des Goldvliesordens: der flämische Ritter de Mamines wurde in Jahre 1430 bei der Belagerung von Melun in diesen Orden eingeweiht. Er trägt besonders ausgeschmückte Turnierausrüstung. **F2** Nach einem Grabbildnis zu Venedig abgebildet: bemerkenswert ist es, dass das Wappen überhaupt nicht auf dem *jupon* erscheint. **F3** Flämischer Ritter aus dem *Livre des Tournois* des 15. Jahrhunderts entnommen.

G1 Aus einem Turnierbuch von der Zeit des Henry VIII von England. **G2** Sizilischer Herold im Diensten des Königs von Aragon: er trägt zur gleichen Zeit die Wappen von Sizilien und Aragon. **G3** Der hier abgebildete Herold ist der *Burggraf* des Kurfürsten von Brandenburg.

H Hier wird Jean de Dillon aus einem zu Arras hergestellten Wandteppich dargestellt. Dort war er *c.*1477 der Beauftragte des Königs von Frankreich. Die Rüstung wird mit keinerlei Wappenkleidung gedeckt und, da Schilder zu dieser Zeit nur selten bei der Schlacht getragen wurden ist die Fahne zum Hauptkennzeichen geworden.